Healthy Habits
Wash and Clean

Sue Barraclough

SEA-TO-SEA
Mankato Collingwood London

This edition first published in 2012 by
Sea-to-Sea Publications
Distributed by Black Rabbit Books
P.O. Box 3263, Mankato, Minnesota 56002
Copyright © Sea-to-Sea Publications 2012
Printed in China

9 8 7 6 5 4 3 2

Published by arrangement with the Watts Publishing
Group Ltd, London.

Library of Congress Cataloging-in-Publication Data

Barraclough, Sue.
 Wash and clean / by Sue Barraclough.
    p. cm. -- (Healthy habits)
 Includes index.
 ISBN 978-1-59771-310-8 (library binding)
 1. Hygiene--Juvenile literature. 2. Grooming behavior in animals--
Juvenile literature. I. Title.
 RA777.B37 2012
 613--dc22

                                            2011001218

Art director: Jonathan Hair
Series editor: Julia Bird
Design: Jane Hawkins

Picture credits: Eric Baccega/Nature PL: 13; Steve Bacon/
Getty Images: 8; BloomImage/Corbis: front cover t;
Bernard Castelein/Nature PL: 6; Gael Conrad/Corbis:4.
Peter Dazely/Getty Images: 11; Holger Ehlers/Alamy: front cover b; Suzi Eszterhas/Minden Pictures/
FLPA Images: 17;
John Fairclough/OSF/Photolibrary: 2, 9; Danny Green/NHPA: 21; Ian Green/NHPA: 18; Hallgerd/
Shutterstock: 7;
Image Source Pink/Alamy: 19; Juice Images/Corbis: 22;
Moodboard/Corbis: 12; Keith Morris/Alamy: 20; Peter Oxford/Nature PL: 10;
José Luis Pelaez/Corbis: 1, 15; Andy Rouse/NHPA: 5; Tom Stewart/Corbis: 16; UpperCut Images/
Alamy: 23. Warren Photographic: 14 (digital reconstruction).

February 2011
RD/6000006415/001

Contents

Washing and Cleaning

Washing and cleaning is something that humans and other animals need to do to stay **healthy**. Washing and cleaning helps protect you against **germs** that cause sickness.

Wash your skin to keep it clean and soft.

Most animals spend time cleaning or washing themselves every day. Many animals use their tongue to lick their skin or fur.

This cheetah is using her tongue to clean her cub.

Body Coverings

Animals have different coverings such as fur, feathers, **scales,** or skin. A covering protects an animal's body so the animal needs to keep it clean and healthy.

A bird needs clean, smooth feathers to keep warm and to fly.

Your skin, hair, and nails cover and protect your body. Washing and cleaning keeps your skin, hair, and nails strong and healthy.

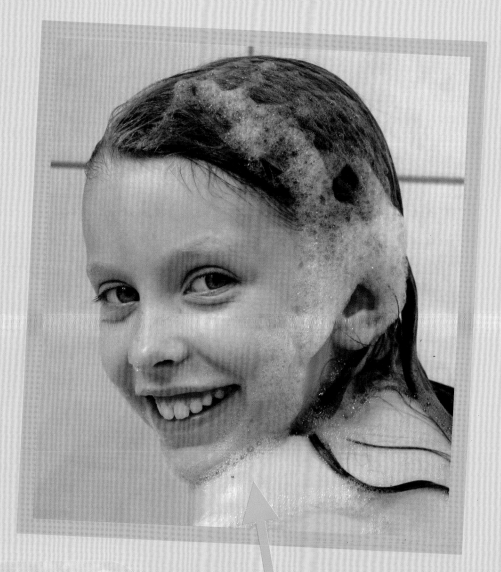

 **What is the largest organ in your body?**

Your skin.

Washing your hair with shampoo keeps it clean and shiny.

Mud and Dust

When you are muddy or dusty you wash to get clean. A shower or bath washes the dirt away.

It can be fun to get muddy in a game!

Think About It

How do you feel when you are dirty?

Many wild animals use mud or dust
to clean and protect their skin. A
layer of mud protects skin from the
Sun. A dust bath gets rid of small
biting insects that can spread germs.

This elephant
has taken a mud
bath in a river.

9

Brushing and Combing

Monkeys and other animals **groom** each other. Monkeys use their fingers to comb through each other's fur, looking for small biting insects.

This adult monkey is checking a younger monkey for insects.

Brushing and combing keeps hair shiny and smooth. If your **scalp** is itchy or sore, you may have a skin problem or **head lice.**

You need help to check your hair for head lice.

Biting and Chewing

You use your teeth to bite and **chew** your food. You need to keep your teeth clean so they stay strong and healthy.

You need strong teeth to bite into a crunchy apple.

Many meat-eating animals have big, sharp teeth. They use their teeth to catch and chew food.

Q Which animal has the biggest teeth?

A The elephant! Its tusks are really part of its teeth.

This bear uses its sharp teeth to catch a fish.

13

Cleaning Teeth

Some crocodiles use birds to help clean their teeth. This crocodile lets a bird peck food from its mouth and teeth.

You brush your teeth to get rid of bits of food and harmful sugar.

You use a toothbrush and toothpaste to keep your teeth clean.

Think About It

Do all animals eat candies and sugary foods?

Brush and Floss

Sometimes brushing does not clean your teeth well enough. Small pieces of food trapped in between your teeth can cause **decay**. As you get older, it is important to **floss** between your teeth, too.

Flossing cleans in between your teeth.

This bear cub is gnawing a bone.

Many animals keep their teeth clean by chewing or **gnawing** things. Wolves and big cats such as lions gnaw bones. Rabbits and horses chew tough grass.

What other animals floss their teeth?

Apes and monkeys. They floss their teeth with pieces of hair.

17

Hands, Nails, Claws

Many animals need to be able to run fast to catch **prey**. Keeping their paws healthy and claws clean and sharp is important.

This tiger scratches a tree to keep its claws sharp and strong.

You use your hands for all kinds of things so it is important to keep them clean. Washing stops the spread of germs that cause sickness. Always wash your hands after going to the bathroom and before you eat.

Think About It

How many times do you wash your hands every day?

Dirt and germs can get trapped under your nails so you should trim them with nail clippers.

Healthy Feet

Feet are an important part of your body. You need strong, healthy feet so you can walk and run.

Dry your feet well to keep the skin healthy. Pay special attention to the skin between your toes!

A rabbit licks its feet to keep them clean and healthy.

All animals need their feet to be healthy so they can walk and run. Many animals need their feet to be healthy so they can run to escape from **predators**.

21

Keeping Clean and Healthy

✓ Hands can spread germs, so wash your hands well:

  • before you eat.

  • after you go to the bathroom.

  • after you touch a pet.

✓ Always wash your hands carefully. Make sure you wash them well all over.

✓ Wash your skin with gentle soap and warm water. Dry with a soft, clean towel.

Always wash your hands after you have gone to the bathroom.

✓ Be careful to keep cuts and broken skin clean. Bandages keep out dirt and germs until your skin heals.

✓ Brush your teeth at least twice a day. When you are about 8 or 9 years old, you can start flossing them too.

✓ Crunchy foods, such as apples, celery, and carrots, can help clean your teeth. They also contain **vitamins** that are good for strong, healthy teeth.

Bandages protect broken skin.

Take Care of Your Skin

- Skin covers your body and keeps it at the right temperature.
- Skin is waterproof and if it is cut or bruised, it can repair itself.
- Skin helps you feel things and protects your insides.

Glossary

chew use your teeth and jaws to break down food.

decay to go bad or rot.

floss use a thread to clean in between teeth.

germ a very small living thing that causes sickness.

gnaw use teeth to bite and crunch food.

groom brush and clean.

head lice small insects that live in hair or fur.

healthy strong and full of energy.

organ a part of a body with a particular job to do.

predator an animal that kills and eats other animals.

prey an animal that is eaten by another animal.

scales tiny, flat pieces of hard material that cover some animals' bodies. Fish and snakes have scaly skin.

scalp the skin on the top of your head.

vitamins one of a group of substances that are found in food.

Index